Excel Basic Skills

Spelling and Vocabulary

3–4 Years

Ages 8-10

Get the Results You Want!

Peter Clutterbuck

PASCAL PRESS

Reprinted 1999, 2001, 2002, 2003, 2004, 2006, 2008, 2009, 2010, 2011 (twice), 2013, 2015, 2017, 2019, 2020 (twice), 2021, 2022, 2023, 2024, 2025

ISBN 978 1 86441 282 6

Pascal Press
PO Box 250
Glebe NSW 2037
www.pascalpress.com.au

Publisher: Vivienne Joannou
Typeset by Grizzly Graphics (Leanne Richters)
Cover by DiZign Pty Ltd
Printed by Vivar Printing/Green Giant Press

About this book

Excel *Basic Skills Spelling and Vocabulary* titles are designed not only to help children improve their spelling skills, but also to widen their knowledge of words.

The activities are simple and self-explanatory, allowing children to work independently within any particular area where they are experiencing difficulty. Answers are provided in a removable answer section.

The book contains all the elements of spelling and vocabulary relevant to Year 3 and Year 4. Parents and teachers will not only be able to direct children to specific activities for which there is a need, but will also obtain ideas for further activities to strengthen and reinforce needed skills.

TABLE OF CONTENTS

DOUBLE LETTERS

Many words that we spell have double letters. It is important to know which double letters to add.

Which set of double letters should be added?
a young dog p u ______ y (bb mm pp)
Answer = pu ***pp*** *y*

Choose the correct double letters to complete each word.

1. The covering of a house is a r______f.

(a) ee (b) oo (c) aa

2. An animal that gives us wool is a sh______p.

(a) ee (b) oo (c) ii

3. A baby cat is a ki______en.

(a) bb (b) tt (c) dd

4. Something sweet to eat is a lo______y.

(a) bb (b) ll (c) tt

5. We boil water in a ke_____le.

(a) tt (b) ll (c) pp

6. We wear a sli______er on our foot.

(a) tt (b) pp (c) ll

7. A rabbit can dig a bu______ow.

(a) ll (b) rr (c) dd

8. An orange root vegetable is a ca______ot.

(a) rr (b) ll (c) tt

9. I hit the nail with a ha______er.

(a) rr (b) ll (c) mm

10. I drank the cola from the bo_____le.

(a) bb (b) ss (c) tt

11. The window is made of gla_____.

(a) bb (b) ss (c) ll

12. My shirt has a dirty co_____ar.

(a) b (b) ll (c) nn

SILENT LETTERS

Some words contain letters that we do not sound when we say them. This can make it difficult for us to spell them.
For example, the word **school** has a silent **-h**.

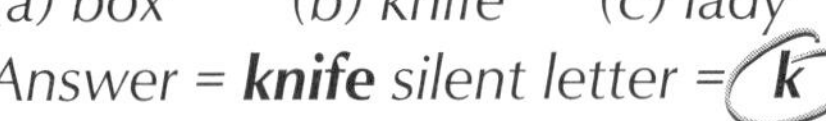

Example

Which of these words has a silent letter and what is it?
(a) box *(b) knife* *(c) lady*
*Answer = **knife** silent letter = (k)*

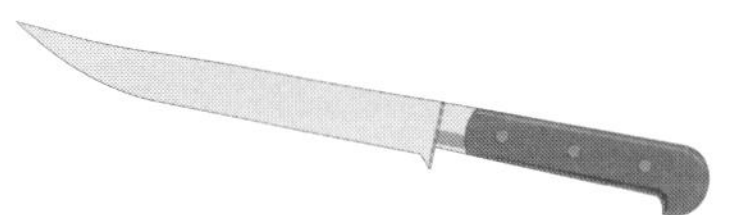

Now do these. Which word contains a silent letter? Write the word and circle the letter that is silent.

1. roof car lamb

____

2. crumb water wind

____

3. ball chair knee

____

4. paper climb bike

____

5. book fish knit

____

6. must hour wing

____

7. comb nest end

____

8. land knew wind

____

9. song wrap away

____

10. ghost paper shop

____

11. most today write

____

12. over palm drum

____

The vowels are *a, e, i, o* and *u*.

Add the missing vowels to make the word.
We caught three fish in the r __ v ___ r.
*Answer = We caught three fish in the r**i**v**e**r.*

Now do these.

1. A cold season of the year is w ____ nt_____r.
2. I ate a juicy _____ppl_____ for my lunch.
3. A ripe banana is always y____ll___w.
4. Dogs like to chew b_____n_____s.
5. When I threw the stone it broke the w_____nd_____w.
6. A baby cat is called a k_____tt_____n.
7. The number after sixty-nine is s_____v_____nty.
8. A furry animal with long ears is a r_____ bb_____t.
9. When something is under other things it is said to be b_____l_____w them.
10. A small ship you can row is called a b_____ _____t.
11. The fat we take from milk and use to make butter is called cr_____ _____m.
12. Links of steel joined together are called a ch_____ _____n.

LETTER PATTERNS

It helps us spell words if we become familiar with the letter patterns that are used to make them.

Example

Which word on the right contains the same letter pattern as the word in bold type?
take *took* *bike* *cake*
Answer = ***cake*** *The pattern is* ***ake***
Remember, the words need not sound the same.

Now do these. Circle the word that contains the same letter pattern and write the pattern on the line.

1. **grade** blast shade song

   ____

2. **card** hard cord pond

   ____

3. **grass** lawn miss class

   ____

4. **brave** shave bride ball

   ____

5. **crash** warm splash behave

   ____

6. **warm** firm worm swarm

   ____

7. **flame** shame time team

   ____

8. **wand** sand rash paper

   ____

9. **gate** cash bark date

   ____

10. **shark** pencil spark fish

    ____

11. **catch** ball match game

    ____

12. **snail** worm flower trail

    ____

To become good spellers we must know the sounds made by groups of letters.

For example, ow = long **o** sound — yell**ow**

ea = long **e** sound — b**ea**n

Choose the correct sound to complete the word.

I fell and hurt my kn________. (oo ee ie)

*Answer = I fell and hurt my kn**ee**.*

Now choose the correct sound unit to fill the spaces.

1. The jumper is made of soft w_____l.
(ee oo ie)

2. If you heat water it will b______l.
(ee oi on)

3. A type of flower is a d______sy.
(oo ai ue)

4. I always pray in ch______ch.
(ar ur ea)

5. An animal with horns is a g______t.
(oa oo ai)

6. Last night I had a scary dr_____m.
(ai ea oo)

7. Hockey is a type of sp_______t.
(ar or er)

8. We made toast from the br______d.
(ea oo ai)

9. A tall building is called a t______er.
(ou ow ar)

10. Sally is wearing a blue sk______t.
(ar ir ie)

11. A type of bird is a h_______k.
(ar or aw)

12. The joint of your arm is called your elb_______.
(or ow ar)

PLURALS

Many spelling difficulties occur because we are not sure how to make words mean more than one *(plural)*.

Most words simply add **-s.**
For example, one **table**—two **tables**, one **shop**—five **shops**

Words that end in **-ch, -sh, -ss, -s,** or **-x** make their plural by adding **-es**.
For example, one **church**—two **churches**, one **fox**—three **foxes**

Make the word in brackets mean more than one.

1. There are six ____________ in the bowl. (apple)

2. We saw five black ____________ at the zoo. (snake)

3. There are seven ____________ in the cupboard. (glass)

4. Katy has two blue ____________. (dress)

5. Oxygen and nitrogen are two types of ____________. (gas)

6. We saw seven ____________ yesterday. (bus)

7. There are six ____________ at our school. (class)

8. Lots of ____________ are growing in the garden. (bush)

9. The teacher put a lot of ____________ on my sums. (cross)

10. I put all the ____________ on the table. (box)

11. I ate two ____________ for my lunch. (peach)

12. Liu is wearing two ______________ on her left arm. (watch)

BEGINNING BLENDS

It is important to know the groups of letters that are used to begin many words.

Example

Look at the letters that begin the words in each line.

st	***st**are*	***st**ar*	***st**ir*
tr	***tr**y*	***tr**ack*	***tr**ick*

Write the group of letters that begin each word.

1. When I go to bed I always have a thick ______anket.
(br bl)

2. Do you like to play ______icket?
(cl cr)

3. Last night I had a strange _____eam.
(cr dr)

4. We can make bread with _____our.
(fl fr)

5. An apple is a type of _____uit.
(fl fr)

6. On cold days I like to wear _____oves.
(gl gr)

7. The frightened child began to _____ ream.
(sc sk)

8. An elephant is big but a mouse is _____ all.
(sm sn)

9. The son of a king and queen is called a ______ince.
(pl pr)

10. Venus and Saturn are two ______anets.
(pl pr)

11. I used the mower to cut the _____ass.
(gr cl)

12. Iain ran up the ______airs.
(st sp)

Certain groups of letters are used to end many words.

For example, look at the letters that complete the words in each row.

nd	ha**nd**	la**nd**	sa**nd**	ba**nd**
lp	gu**lp**	he**lp**	ye**lp**	ke**lp**

Example

Add the letters that complete the word.
The bird built a large ne_____. (nd st)
*Answer = The bird built a large ne**st**.*

Now do these the same way.

1. Tom and I both sit at this de_____.
(ct sk)

2. The noise of a pig is called a gru_____.
(st nt)

3. We caught some tadpoles in the po_____.
(nd mp)

4. A kangaroo likes to ju_____.
(nt mp)

5. This old knife is quite blu_____.
(st nt)

6. I gave the hungry dog the cru_____.
(nd st)

7. Last night we had a very cold fro_____.
(sk st)

8. If you heat ice it will me_____.
(lp lt)

9. When he lost his puppy the small boy we_____.
(ct pt)

10. On my face I wore a ma_____.
(st sk)

11. The opposite of right is le_____.
(nd ft)

12. Sheep's wool is very so_____.
(ft nt)

WORD PATTERNS

The shapes of the letters of a word make a pattern.

For example, the letters of **four** make the pattern. f o u r

The letters of **sock** make the pattern. s o c k

Look at the words in the box. Write each in its correct pattern below.

my	sty	ball	rat	moon	home
had	dog	bus	stop	old	ship

1.

2.

3.

4.

5.

6.

7.

8.

9.

10.

11.

12.

SPELLING RULES 1

Certain rules help us learn to spell many words.

When we add **-ing** to the end of a word we often do not have to make any changes.
For example, play — playing

If we add **-ing** to a word that ends in a silent **-e** we drop the **-e** before adding **-ing**.
For example, shine — shining

Add **-ing** to the word in the brackets and write it.
Jo is ________________ me her new bicycle. (show)
Answer = Jo is ***showing*** *me her new bicycle.*

I am ________________ a bicycle. (ride)
Answer = I am ***riding*** *a bicycle.*

Now do these.

1. Jan is ________________ some water. (drink)

2. We are ________________ for the lost watch. (look)

3. The dog is ________________ the stranger. (bite)

4. I am ________________ the path. (sweep)

5. The cook is ________________ a cake. (bake)

6. We are ________________ to our friends. (wave)

7. Nguyen is ________________ the cake. (ice)

8. Tom is ________________ pizza for lunch. (eat)

9. I am ________________ my clothes. (change)

10. The monkey is ________________ the tree. (climb)

11. The dog is ________________ the cat. (chase)

12. The ship is ________________ beneath the water. (sink)

When we add *-ed* or *-ing* to many words we do not have to make any changes.
For example, wash — washed — washing

However, for words that end in a short vowel and one consonant, we double the consonant. For example, drop — dropped — dropping

Add **-ed** or **-ing** to the word and write it.
Mike is ___________ the glass. (drop)
Mike is ***dropping*** *the glass.*
Mike ***dropped*** *the glass.*

Now do these.

1. Mel _______________ me her new bicycle. (show)
2. Matt is _______________ his hair. (brush)
3. The car _______________ at the corner. (stop)
4. Effy is _______________ her hands together. (rub)
5. The kangaroo _______________ over the fence. (hop)
6. The cricketer _______________ the catch. (drop)
7. The frightened children _______________ into the room. (rush)
8. Joe is _______________ the pram. (push)
9. We _______________ football yesterday. (play)
10. We _______________ the chairs into the room. (drag)
11. Tommy is _______________ up the meat. (chop)
12. My mother and I went _______________ last night. (shop)

BASE WORDS

We can add letters to the front or the end of many words.

For example, from the word **dine** we can add **-ing – dining** or to the base word **health** we can add **un** and **y** to make **unhealthy.**

Write the **base** word from which the bold word comes.
*Mike is **hopping** across the yard.*
*Answer = **hop***

Now do these the same way.

1. Wendy is **playing** in the gymnasium.

   ____

2. We are **watching** television.

   ____

3. The thief is **stealing** the jewels.

   ____

4. The dog **barked** at the stranger.

   ____

5. Con isn't **feeling** very well today.

   ____

6. The monkey is **climbing** the tree.

   ____

7. Mary is **riding** her bike to school.

   ____

8. Mr Smith is **baking** a cake.

   ____

9. The large wolf is **chasing** the small deer.

   ____

10. Caitlin is **chopping** the wood.

    ____

11. Paul **stepped** on the broken glass.

    ____

12. These clothes are still **unwashed.**

    ____

It helps us spell words if we know they are made up of different parts. These parts are called the *prefix*, the *base word* and the *suffix*.

Example

Combine the word parts to fit the sentence.

Eating too much meat is ________________ for you.
(un + health + y)
prefix base word suffix
*Answer = Eating too much meat is **unhealthy** for you.*

Now do these the same way. Circle the prefix or suffix.

1. The ________________ painted the picture.
(art + ist)

2. That was a ________________ thing to do.
(fool + ish)

3. The birds flew away ________________.
(swift + ly)

4. The old coins are now ________________.
(worth + less)

5. When they could not find the lost kitten the children felt ________________.
(hope + less)

6. I spoke to John on the ________________.
(tele + phone)

7. Another name for noon is ________________.
(mid + day)

8. I think the teacher was ________________ to Sarah.
(un + fair)

9. I began to ________________ the string around the parcel.
(un + tie)

10. The door is ________________.
(un + lock + ed)

11. The carpenters are ________________ the house.
(re + build + ing)

12. These big rocks are ________________.
(un + crush + ed)

UNIT 14 SYLLABLES YEAR 3

Every syllable contains a vowel sound. The vowels are a, e, i, o and u. Sometimes y is used as a vowel.

Arrange the syllables in order to fit the sentence.
It was a ____________ sunny day. (beau ful ti)
Answer = It was a ***beautiful*** *sunny day.*

It was a beautiful ____________ day. (ny sun)
Answer = It was a beautiful ***sunny*** *day.*

Now do these.

1. When I visited the seaside I spoke to a ____________. (man er fish)

2. I looked up the day and date on the ____________. (en cal dar)

3. It was a ____________ thing that Bill did for us. (der won ful)

4. I had a drink of some fizzy ____________. (on lem ade)

5. The ____________ soon arrived at the place where the cars had crashed. (lance am bu)

6. The story ____________ with a surprise ending. (con clu ded)

7. I put the letter in the ____________. (vel en ope)

8. We took some photographs with the ____________. (a er cam)

9. I am going away for a ____________ next week. (i hol day)

10. We went swimming ____________. (ter yes day)

11. This ____________ we are going for a picnic in the park. (ing e ven)

12. George bought me a large ____________. (lol pop li)

It is important to be able to recognise whether a word is spelt correctly, simply by looking at it.

Proof reading is an important skill to develop if we are to become good spellers.

Choose the correct spelling of the word.
A zebra is ________ and white. (blak black)
Answer = A zebra is ***black*** *and white.*

Now do these the same way.

1. She said she would be __________ by seven o'clock.
   (heer here)

2. Are you __________ to the football tomorrow?
   (going goin)

3. Bill was _____________ across the yard when he tripped.
   (running runing)

4. Would you like some __________ cake?
   (more moor)

5. Josie __________ she would go to the party.
   (siad said)

6. We are going to the movies __________.
   (tonite tonight)

7. Bill is a boy and Susan is a __________.
   (gril girl)

8. This flower is __________ than the one you have.
   (beter better)

9. Dave was punched on the __________.
   (knose nose)

10. I am sure the story he told me is __________.
    (trew true)

11. These muddy clothes are very __________.
    (durty dirty)

12. I am sure the story is __________ snakes.
    (abowt about)

DEMON WORDS

Some words constantly cause us spelling difficulties. We call these Demon Words.

Example

Choose the correct spelling of the Demon Words.
I catch a bus to school ______________ day of the week.
(evry every)
Answer = I catch a bus to school ***every*** *day of the week.*

Now do these the same way.

1. When she fell, Stella ____________ her leg. (hert hurt)

2. That is ____________ car in the garage. (their thier)

3. We must wait here ____________ the rain stops. (untill until)

4. Bill came last and Sharon came ____________ in the race. (first frist)

5. It is ____________ seven o'clock. (allmost almost)

6. Would you like ____________ more cake? (sum some)

7. He said ____________ would all be here soon. (thay they)

8. I ____________ my parents if I could go. (asked arsked)

9. She ____________ she would be here. (sed said)

10. Did you ____________ the thunder? (heer hear)

11. Nick received a nasty knock on the ____________. (hed head)

12. The number after thirty-nine is ____________. (fourty forty)

WORD BUILDING

If we are given sets of letters we can make words by linking them together.

Example

Look at these letter pairs. Use them to make words that fit the meanings.
(be fi ll sh)
a water creature
it rings
Answer = ***fish*** *and* ***bell***

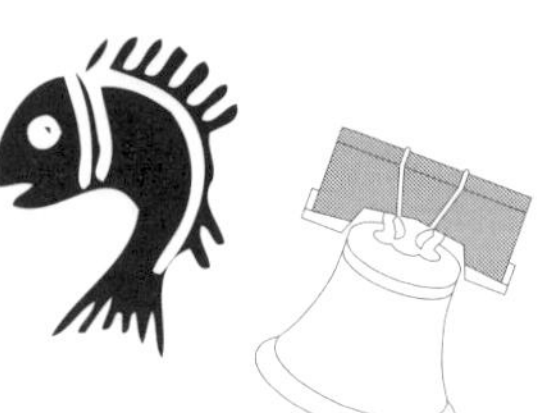

Now add the letter pairs to make two words to fit the meanings given.

1. (bo tr ok ee)
we read it ___________
large plant ___________

2. (sh do ip wn)
it goes across water ___________
opposite of up ___________

3. (mi ba lk ll)
it bounces ___________
it comes from cows ___________

4. (co ba by at)
small child ___________
we wear it ___________

5. (bi so ft rd)
it has feathers ___________
not hard ___________

6. (fo ur th in)
number ___________
not fat ___________

7. (st bo ne ar)
dogs like to chew them ___________
it twinkles at night ___________

8. (pi ye nk ar)
colour ___________
twelve months ___________

9. (no fa se st)
you breathe through it ___________
very quick ___________

10. (ci ty ap so)
large town ___________
for washing ___________

11. (ta ca me ke)
not wild ___________
something to eat ___________

12. (la sl mb ow)
not fast ___________
young sheep ___________

USING A DICTIONARY

A dictionary is a useful tool to help us develop spelling skills. We should all learn how to use one. Remember the words in a dictionary are placed in alphabetical order.

Example

Use your dictionary to add the missing letters.
An animal like a deer is an ***ant*___________.
Answer = An animal like a deer is an ***antelope***.

Now use your dictionary to help you write these words.

1. The day you were born is called your bir___________.

2. Another name for a young sheep is a la___________.

3. We sew bu___________ onto our shirts.

4. A food made from milk is called che___________.

5. The home of a horse is a st___________.

6. A container for water is called a bu___________.

7. A black and white bird that cannot fly is called a pen ___________.

8. An animal that has a very long neck is called a gir___________.

9. A very large number is a mill___________.

10. A break from school is called a hol___________.

11. A very tall hill is called a moun___________.

12. A food made by bees is called hon ___________.

SMALL WORDS

Many large words contain smaller words. Recognising these helps us learn to spell larger words more easily.

Find the smaller word that matches the meaning given.

vanilla (not well)
Answer = ***ill***

Now do these.

1. elephant (an insect)

____

2. spear (a fruit)

____

3. start (a small cake)

____

4. heard (part of the body)

____

5. plumage (a fruit)

____

6. escape (something worn over the head)

____

7. address (something to wear)

____

8. bracelet (speed contest)

____

9. elated (not early)

____

10. abandon (group of musicians)

____

11. tomatoes (floor covering)

____

12. orchestra (part of the body)

____

Even if you know how to spell a word correctly it is important to also know its meaning so you can use it correctly.

Circle the word that has the same meaning.
To yell loudly means to
(a) laugh (b) drive (c) shout
Answer = shout

Now do these.

1. A food made from flour is
(a) fruit (b) bread (c) meat

2. A device that tells us the time is a
(a) clock (b) chair (c) shell

3. Things we wear on our feet are called
(a) horses (b) gloves (c) shoes

4. A small grey-coloured animal is a
(a) house (b) elephant (c) mouse

5. Part of your body is called your
(a) head (b) engine (c) bicycle

6. A small ship is called a
(a) tricycle (b) soap (c) boat

7. A circle is
(a) square (b) round (c) happy

8. We grow flowers in a
(a) paper (b) danger (c) garden

9. You put food in your
(a) mouth (b) ears (c) boots

10. An engine and carriages is called a
(a) train (b) again (c) brain

11. A cow provides us with
(a) silk (b) milk (c) wool

12. Dogs like to chew
(a) bones (b) cones (c) stones

ANAGRAMS

Anagrams are words we make by rearranging all the letters of another word.

Rearrange the letters to make a word that fits the sentence.
Last night a bright __________ was twinkling. (rats)
*Answer = Last night a bright **star** was twinkling.*

Now do these.

1. I was happy when my __________ had kittens. (act)

2. Would you please turn on the __________? (pat)

3. The __________ laid its eggs in the tree. (low)

4. Do you know __________ to shoe a horse? (who)

5. The __________ took the food to its home. (tan)

6. The hair on a horse's neck is called a __________. (mean)

7. I ate a __________ for lunch. (nub)

8. I cooked all the eggs in the frying __________. (nap)

9. I washed the clothes in the __________. (but)

10. Do you know what __________ it is? (emit)

11. I put the cereal into the __________. (blow)

12. I hurt my __________ yesterday. (ram)

HOMOPHONES

Homophones are words that sound the same but are spelt differently. We often know how to spell them but are not sure which one to use.

Example

Circle the correct word to use.
I could not ________ what she said. (hear here)
Answer = I could not ***hear*** *what she said.*

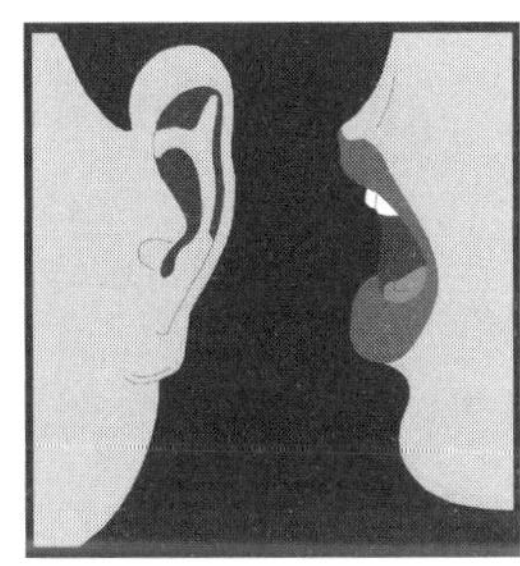

Now do these. Write the correct word in the space.

1. The ________ is shining brightly.
(sun son)

2. The dog wagged its ________ when I gave it the bone. (tale tail)

3. The brick hurt my big ________ when it fell on it. (toe tow)

4. My mother bought me a ________ pair of shoes. (knew new)

5. Have you ever ________ to London?
(bean been)

6. I am going to ________ some lollies with the dollar you gave me.
(buy by)

7. Last night I ________ a very strange bird.
(saw sore)

8. This old ________ is very bumpy.
(rode road)

9. Do you know ________ pen is yours?
(which witch)

10. Did you ________ Billy?
(see sea)

11. The large, brown ________ chased the hunter away from its cub.
(bare bear)

12. Last ________ our class went on an excursion to the zoo.
(week weak)

ANTONYMS

Antonyms are words that have the opposite, or nearly the opposite, meaning.

Example

Which word is opposite in meaning to the bold word?
*This flag is **white** but that one is ________.*
(dull silly black)
*Answer = This flag is white but that one is **black.***

Now choose the opposite of the bold word from the words in brackets.

1. Bill is **good** but Mary is ________.
(silly bad old)

2. Sally is a **girl** but Tom is a ________.
(boy cat book)

3. Today it is **hot** but yesterday it was ________.
(blue cold new)

4. This door is **open** but that one is ________.
(hot glad shut)

5. A rock is **hard** but my pillow is ________.
(close pretty soft)

6. Freya is at the **front** and Ned is at the ________ of the room.
(kind close back)

7. Tom is **awake** but Jack is still ________.
(asleep crying eating)

8. Andy came **first** and I came ________ in the race.
(last thin glad)

9. This pig is **thin** but that one is ________.
(old red fat)

10. The road **starts** here and ________ over there.
(races ends loses)

11. The clock is **above** the table but the box is ________ it.
(near under soon)

12. An elephant is **big** but a mouse is ________.
(tall little silly)

Synonyms are words that have the same, or nearly the same, meanings.

Circle the word that has the same meaning as the bold word.
*I cleaned the **mat** on the floor.*
(basket rug saucer)
*Answer = **rug***

Now circle the word in brackets that has the same, or nearly the same, meaning as the bold word.

1. There was a large **rock** on the footpath.
   (cow stone bike)

2. I am **happy** she is here.
   (sad glad ill)

3. We had a swim in the **ocean**.
   (sea sand bush)

4. Please **close** that door now.
   (help paint shut)

5. Stuart is a very **fast** runner.
   (slow tired quick)

6. On the farm there is a **pony.**
   (dog pig horse)

7. When he lost his jumper the boy began to **cry**.
   (laugh weep run)

8. I put the fruit in the glass **bowl.**
   (dish bucket spade)

9. Will is a new **student** at our school.
   (pupil book television)

10. My bedroom is always **tidy**.
    (cold neat dirty)

11. Chan is a very strong **lad**.
    (tree boy arm)

12. The cups on the table began to **fall** off.
    (play come drop)

SIMILES

Similes are groups of words used to compare two things. Words such as *as* or *like* are used to make the comparison.

Which word best completes the sentence?

Billy has been as busy as a ____________ all this week.

(pig cat bee)

Answer = Billy has been as busy as a ***bee*** *all this week.*

Now do these.

1. The weather has been as cold as ____________ this week.
   (five ice stone)

2. My Mum looked as pretty as an ____________.
   (angel ice-cream elephant)

3. His sneezes sounded like a ____________.
   (machine gun truck cold)

4. This new pillow is as soft as a ____________.
   (marshmallow toffee apple sleepy)

5. The sun today is as hot as ____________.
   (ice fire paper)

6. When I run I am as fast as a ____________.
   (puppy leopard bee)

7. The fireworks sounded like ____________.
   (crackers cannons cars)

8. This pig is fat but that one is like a ____________.
   (stick piglet tub)

Now try making up your own. You can use more than one word.

9. The squashed pizza looked like __________________.

10. The spider was as hairy as __________________.

11. The present made me as happy as __________________.

12. My sister's haircut looked like __________________.

UNIT 26 — PLACES — YEAR 3

Where do people or animals live? Where are things kept? Where do we buy things?

Example

Which word best completes the sentence?
A king lives in a ________. (web shed castle)
Answer = A king lives in a ***castle****.*

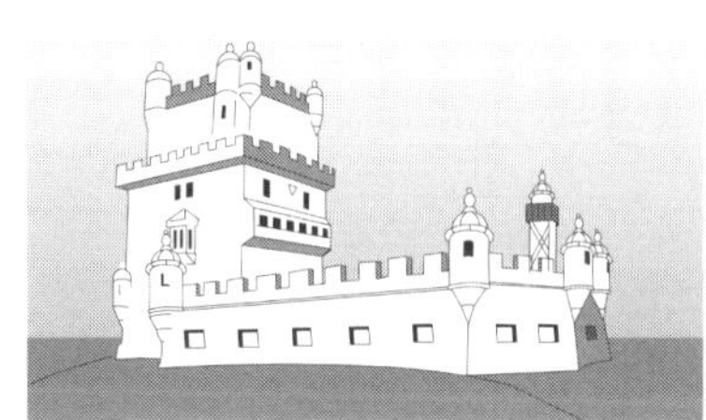

Now do these.

1. I put the puppy back in its ____________.
(kennel hive nest)

2. There are four horses in the ____________.
(kitchen stable cot)

3. I bought a loaf of bread at the ____________.
(library bakery chemist)

4. I borrowed a book from the ____________.
(stable kennel library)

5. My mother parked the car in the ____________.
(bedroom garage box)

6. The train stopped at the ____________.
(station hive kitchen)

7. The large jets landed at the ____________.
(airport station bedroom)

8. All the bees are back in their ____________.
(nest hive web)

9. The baby is sleeping in its ____________.
(cot hive nest)

10. We picked the flowers that were growing in the ____________.
(garden bathroom dam)

11. Last evening we went for a picnic in the ____________.
(garage hospital park)

12. James and I made sandcastles at the ____________.
(factory bed beach)

UNIT 27 — COMPOUND WORDS — YEAR 3

Compound words are made up of two or more smaller words.

Example

Which word best completes the bold word?
We looked at the ***water*** ________.
(mat dog fall)
Answer = We looked at the ***waterfall****.*

Now do these the same way.

1. The policeman took the lady's **finger**____________.
(toes prints stops)

2. For lunch I ate a large **grape** ____________.
(bone fruit coat)

3. When it is cold I always wear an **over** ____________.
(socks coat shirt)

4. The table is covered with a pink **table**____________.
(apron cloth lolly)

5. I have just finished reading the **news**____________.
(book paper pen)

6. What are you doing this **after**____________?
(lunch noon night)

7. The sailors saw the beam of the **light**____________.
(house roads cloth)

8. In the playground there was a **grass**____________.
(ant hopper horse)

9. Next week we are going on holidays to the **sea**____________.
(side bucket room)

10. After breakfast I washed the **egg** ____________.
(spoon table cup)

11. When we were at the beach I saw a **jelly**____________.
(dog pen fish)

12. Mrs Smith is my **grand**____________.
(book fish mother)

PEOPLE

People can be called different names according to their job or the role they are playing.

Which word correctly fills the space?
The ___________ helped me with my spelling.
(pilot teacher king)
Answer = ***teacher***

Now do these.

1. The ____________ took my blood pressure and listened to my heartbeat.

   (mother plumber doctor)

2. The ____________ mended the leaking taps in our kitchen.

   (teacher plumber nurse)

3. The ____________ flew the large jet overseas.

   (pirate queen pilot)

4. The ____________ painted a picture of the town.

   (judge artist pilot)

5. The ___________ harvested the crop of wheat.

   (doctor dentist farmer)

6. I bought some medication from the ____________.

   (chemist florist postman)

7. The ____________ at the circus make us laugh.

   (grocers clowns sailors)

8. The factory ____________ warned the men to keep out.

   (king baby guard)

9. The __________ has finished the large house in our street.

   (doctor tailor builder)

10. The ________ sold us some tender meat.

    (tailor butcher artist)

11. We bought the flowers at the ___________ shop.

    (florist nurse clown)

12. The __________ rode the horse.

    (dentist soldier jockey)

UNIT 29 ONE WORD FOR MANY YEAR 3

Often we use a group of words when one word would do.

Which word could replace the bold words in the sentence?
When we were at the beach I saw a ***small sea creature.***
(camel crab apple)
Answer = crab

Now circle the word which could replace the bold words in each sentence.

1. I threw the **bits of bread** to the hungry birds.
(twigs crumbs boxes)

2. Margaret **chewed loudly** when she ate the apple.
(munched boxed skipped)

3. I put the **frozen water** in the glass.
(fire table ice)

4. When the dog bit him Chris began to **shake with fear**.
(laugh tremble skip)

5. When I was in bed I heard a **dull sound**.
(laugh tremble thud)

6. The man is now **able to do as he pleases**.
(old ill free)

7. Yesterday there were lots of **young boys and girls** in the park.
(rabbits tables children)

8. My dad bought a new **small bed for a baby**.
(car cot bike)

9. That dog is **very small**.
(big old tiny)

10. My uncle is **not able to see**.
(blind old sick)

11. The farmer stashed the **dried grass** in the shed.
(straw stones cows)

12. Mira was **in front** of the other children.
(behind ahead between)

Many words we use can be placed into a group.

Example

Which word on the right belongs with the bold words on the left?
eye nose mouth ____________ *(arm ear toe)*
Answer = **ear** *as it is also on your head.*

Now write the word that belongs to the same group.

1. bee ant wasp ____________
(cow beetle table)

2. blue green yellow ____________
(brown table saucer)

3. magpie emu duck ____________
(camel canary apricot)

4. Tuesday Thursday Monday
____
(Joan Wednesday April)

5. boots slippers thongs ____________
(hats jumpers shoes)

6. beans carrots peas ____________
(books apples potatoes)

7. apple banana apricot ____________
(frock milk lemon)

8. chair stool sofa ____________
(table road pencil)

9. tulip daisy violet ____________
(cow rose tomato)

10. stable kennel hive
____
(chair nest flower)

11. fifty ninety thirteen ____________
(banana seventy desk)

12. cup plate saucer ____________
(bowl bath bed)

RHYMING WORDS

When words make the same sound we say that they rhyme.

Example

Which word sounds the same as the bold word?
*A word that sounds the same as **gun** is __________. (jog run tune)*
*Answer = **run***

Remember that words don't have to look the same to sound the same.

Now do these the same way. Write the rhyming word in the space.

1. A word that rhymes with **sink** is __________.
(drank think gale)

2. A word that rhymes with **thin** is __________.
(fat fine bin)

3. A word that rhymes with **bite** is __________.
(fight nip teeth)

4. A word that rhymes with **meat** is __________.
(food team feet)

5. A word that rhymes with **lost** is __________.
(most cost coat)

6. A word that rhymes with **nest** is __________.
(fist rest tent)

7. A word that rhymes with **her** is __________.
(fur egg hen)

8. A word that rhymes with **said** is __________.
(ship train bed)

9. A word that rhymes with **sky** is __________.
(cloud skin pie)

10. A word that rhymes with **door** is __________.
(spoon moon poor)

11. A word that rhymes with **sleep** is __________.
(cheap awake team)

12. A word that rhymes with **look** is __________.
(pool leek book)

UNIT 1

1. oo
2. ee
3. tt
4. ll
5. tt
6. pp
7. rr
8. rr
9. mm
10. tt
11. ss
12. ll

UNIT 2

1. lam**b**
2. crum**b**
3. **k**nee
4. clim**b**
5. **k**nit
6. **h**our
7. com**b**
8. **k**new
9. **w**rap
10. g**h**ost
11. **w**rite
12. pa**l**m

UNIT 3

1. w**i**nt**e**r
2. **a**ppl**e**
3. y**e**ll**o**w
4. b**o**n**e**s
5. w**i**nd**o**w
6. k**i**tt**e**n
7. s**e**v**e**nty
8. r**a**bb**i**t
9. b**e**l**o**w
10. b**oa**t
11. cr**ea**m
12. ch**ai**n

UNIT 4

1. sh**ade**
2. h**ard**
3. cl**ass**
4. sh**ave**
5. spl**ash**
6. sw**arm**
7. sh**ame**
8. s**and**
9. d**ate**
10. sp**ark**
11. m**atch**
12. tr**ail**

UNIT 5

1. oo
2. oi
3. ai
4. ur
5. oa
6. ea
7. or
8. ea
9. ow
10. ir
11. aw
12. ow

UNIT 6

1. apples
2. snakes
3. glasses
4. dresses
5. gases
6. buses
7. classes
8. bushes
9. crosses
10. boxes
11. peaches
12. watches

UNIT 7

1. bl
2. cr
3. dr
4. fl
5. fr
6. gl
7. sc
8. sm
9. pr
10. pl
11. gr
12. st

UNIT 8

1. sk
2. nt
3. nd
4. mp
5. nt
6. st
7. st
8. lt
9. pt
10. sk
11. ft
12. ft

UNIT 9

1. rat
2. home
3. ball
4. my
5. had
6. stop
7. old
8. moon
9. ship
10. bus
11. dog
12. sty

UNIT 10

1. drinking
2. looking
3. biting
4. sweeping
5. baking
6. waving
7. icing
8. eating
9. changing
10. climbing
11. chasing
12. sinking

UNIT 11

1. showed
2. brushing
3. stopped
4. rubbing
5. hopped
6. dropped
7. rushed
8. pushing
9. played
10. dragged
11. chopping
12. shopping

UNIT 12

1. play
2. watch
3. steal
4. bark
5. feel
6. climb
7. ride
8. bake
9. chase
10. chop
11. step
12. wash

UNIT 13

1. art**ist**
2. fool**ish**
3. swift**ly**
4. worth**less**
5. hope**less**
6. **tele**phone
7. **mid**day
8. **un**fair
9. **un**tie
10. **un**lock**ed**
11. **re**build**ing**
12. **un**crush**ed**

UNIT 14

1. fisherman
2. calendar
3. wonderful
4. lemonade
5. ambulance
6. concluded
7. envelope
8. camera
9. holiday
10. yesterday
11. evening
12. lollipop

UNIT 15

1. here
2. going
3. running
4. more
5. said
6. tonight
7. girl
8. better
9. nose
10. true
11. dirty
12. about

UNIT 16

1. hurt
2. their
3. until
4. first
5. almost
6. some
7. they
8. asked
9. said
10. hear
11. head
12. forty

UNIT 17

1. book, tree 2. ship, down 3. ball, milk
4. baby, coat 5. bird, soft 6. four, thin
7. bone, star 8. pink, year 9. nose, fast
10. city, soap 11. tame, cake 12. slow, lamb

UNIT 18

1. birthday 2. lamb 3. buttons
4. cheese 5. stable 6. bucket
7. penguin 8. giraffe 9. million
10. holiday 11. mountain 12. honey

UNIT 19

1. ant 2. pear 3. tart
4. ear 5. plum 6. cap
7. dress 8. race 9. late
10. band 11. mat 12. chest

UNIT 20

1. bread 2. clock 3. shoes
4. mouse 5. head 6. boat
7. round 8. garden 9. mouth
10. train 11. milk 12. bones

UNIT 21

1. cat 2. tap 3. owl
4. how 5. ant 6. mane
7. bun 8. pan 9. tub
10. time 11. bowl 12. arm

UNIT 22

1. sun 2. tail 3. toe
4. new 5. been 6. buy
7. saw 8. road 9. which
10. see 11. bear 12. week

UNIT 23

1. bad 2. boy 3. cold
4. shut 5. soft 6. back
7. asleep 8. last 9. fat
10. ends 11. under 12. little

UNIT 24

1. stone 2. glad 3. sea
4. shut 5. quick 6. horse
7. weep 8. dish 9. pupil
10. neat 11. boy 12. drop

UNIT 25

1. ice 2. angel 3. machine gun
4. marshmallow 5. fire 6. leopard
7. cannons 8. stick
9. – 12. Answers will vary.

UNIT 26

1. kennel 2. stable 3. bakery
4. library 5. garage 6. station
7. airport 8. hive 9. cot
10. garden 11. park 12. beach

UNIT 27

1. prints 2. fruit 3. coat
4. cloth 5. paper 6. noon
7. house 8. hopper 9. side
10. cup 11. fish 12. mother

UNIT 28

1. doctor 2. plumber 3. pilot
4. artist 5. farmer 6. chemist
7. clowns 8. guard 9. builder
10. butcher 11. florist 12. jockey

UNIT 29

1. crumbs 2. munched 3. ice
4. tremble 5. thud 6. free
7. children 8. cot 9. tiny
10. blind 11. straw 12. ahead

UNIT 30

1. beetle 2. brown 3. canary
4. Wednesday 5. shoes 6. potatoes
7. lemon 8. table 9. rose
10. nest 11. seventy 12. bowl

UNIT 31

1. think 2. bin 3. fight
4. feet 5. cost 6. rest
7. fur 8. bed 9. pie
10. poor 11. cheap 12. book

MASTERY TEST

1. pu**pp**y 2. lam**b** 3. f**i**ng**e**r
4. b**ones** 5. sh**ar**k 6. bushes
7. **br**ead 8. ma**sk**
9. rubb**ed**, rubbi**ng** 10. bake 11. unopened
12. lemonade 13. blue 14. hand, year
15. apri**cot** 16. rat
17. square 18. see 19. back
20. warm 21. snow 22. bakery
23. stack 24. clown 25. sad
26. pig 27. go

UNIT 1
1. ll
2. rr
3. dd
4. rr
5. ll
6. pp
7. dd
8. tt
9. pp
10. ss
11. tt
12. nn

UNIT 2
1. hour
2. knife
3. crumb
4. calf
5. wrap
6. know
7. palm
8. wrong
9. lamb
10. limb
11. castle
12. write

UNIT 3
1. sister
2. pulled
3. stable
4. brought
5. donkey
6. bucket
7. pocket
8. factory
9. ladder
10. bottom
11. holiday
12. animal

UNIT 4
1. dead
2. beach
3. thrash
4. spend
5. stare
6. stool
7. coast
8. money
9. morning
10. whose
11. ground
12. almost

UNIT 5
1. choose
2. steel
3. morning
4. cream
5. silver
6. enjoy
7. toast
8. afraid
9. crayon
10. speech
11. straw
12. thirsty

UNIT 6
1. apples
2. bunches
3. dishes
4. glasses
5. buses
6. turkeys
7. stories
8. poppies
9. toys
10. foxes
11. wishes
12. matches

UNIT 7
1. st
2. sp
3. sn
4. sw
5. tw
6. fl
7. gr
8. pr
9. sc
10. dr
11. cr
12. bl

UNIT 8
1. mp
2. pt
3. nt
4. lt
5. ct
6. nt
7. sk
8. ft
9. st
10. ne
11. nt
12. ct

UNIT 9
1. blue (or thin)
2. mouse
3. thin (or blue)
4. bark
5. shell
6. place
7. black
8. sick
9. four
10. park
11. white
12. frog

UNIT 10
1. cooked
2. showed
3. looked
4. wished
5. liked
6. chased
7. changed
8. dragged
9. watched
10. stopped
11. rubbed
12. trotted

UNIT 11
1. meeting
2. doing
3. singing
4. riding
5. making
6. hiding
7. skipping
8. humming
9. swimming
10. cutting
11. shopping
12. putting

UNIT 12
1. ride
2. watch
3. stop
4. weep
5. curl
6. come
7. wash
8. door
9. end
10. want
11. red
12. spoon

UNIT 13
1. unsuccessful
2. unhealthy
3. unwashed
4. imprisoned
5. indoors
6. explained
7. uncooked
8. unfinished
9. unwilling
10. unsteady
11. unclaimed
12. rebuilding

UNIT 14
1. animal
2. dangerous
3. adventure
4. continue
5. magazine
6. telephone
7. mosquito
8. runaway
9. tomorrow
10. introduce
11. November
12. replaces

UNIT 15
1. letter
2. many
3. every
4. dropped
5. wool
6. apple
7. once
8. some
9. across
10. clock
11. train
12. bird

UNIT 16
1. which
2. always
3. piece
4. because
5. cotton
6. forty
7. swimming
8. almost
9. coming
10. school
11. might
12. tried

UNIT 17

1. camel	2. bear	3. fleet
4. stop	5. first	6. frog
7. fast	8. stream	9. ship
10. coat	11. nest	12. boat

UNIT 18

1. basket	2. gander	3. blanket
4. mistake	5. insect	6. saucer
7. piano	8. feathers	9. chimney
10. giant	11. question	12. pencil

UNIT 19

1. give book	2. fish frog	3. ball doll
4. hand foot	5. wool milk	6. game yard
7. gold ring	8. coat shop	9. boat ship
10. farm duck	11. pear cake	12. mice trap

UNIT 20

1. nurse	2. captain	3. honey
4. giant	5. helmet	6. cherry
7. daisy	8. match	9. menu
10. octopus	11. pedal	12. saddle

UNIT 21

1. tea	2. came	3. paws
4. post	5. race	6. rats
7. wolf	8. lame	9. pear
10. seat	11. rose	12. table

UNIT 22

1. mail	2. hare	3. poor
4. peel	5. bury	6. hole
7. threw	8. meet	9. break
10. rose	11. horse	12. deer

UNIT 23

1. dead	2. bright	3. cruel
4. smooth	5. weak	6. shallow
7. shut	8. bald	9. straight
10. dirty	11. going	12. lost

UNIT 24

1. allow	2. wet	3. stupid
4. scent	5. scare	6. round
7. price	8. fix	9. start
10. edge	11. present	12. find

UNIT 25

1. buildings	2. night	3. baby
4. jewels	5. thunder	6. ghosts
7. rocks	8. sand	

9.–12. Answers will vary.

UNIT 26

1. envelope	2. nest	3. kettle
4. carton	5. wardrobe	6. purse
7. kitchen	8. dictionary	9. silo
10. bottle	11. zoo	12. supermarket

UNIT 27

1. paste	2. box	3. ship
4. dog	5. lace	6. board
7. ball	8. work	9. port
10. fall	11. cake	12. path

UNIT 28

1. dentist	2. cashier	3. conductor
4. butcher	5. bully	6. judge
7. detective	8. blacksmith	9. umpire
10. sailor	11. nurse	12. tailor

UNIT 29

1. late	2. sad	3. add
4. cleaned	5. ground	6. next
7. exit	8. hurry	9. ugly
10. enough	11. crowd	12. lane

UNIT 30

1. fly	2. emu	3. copper
4. orange	5. truck	6. soccer
7. snow	8. beans	9. tie
10. knee	11. spoon	12. bowl

UNIT 31

1. (a) bark (b) bark	2. (a) rock (b) rock	3. (a) sink (b) sink
4. (a) bank (b) bank	5. (a) match (b) match	6. (a) trip (b) trip

MASTERY TEST

1. jelly	2. palm	3. winter
4. pear	5. chain	6. bunches
7. brown	8. stamp	
9. chased, chasing		10. stop
11. understood	12. yesterday	13. swimming
14. string	15. goanna	16. tree, bird
17. foal	18. wolf	19. here
20. dull	21. neat	22. ice
23. garage	24. windmill	25. dentist
26. bald	27. emu	

28. Answers will vary but should include bank as in riverside and as in financial institution. They can also include bank as in an aeroplane turning whilst in flight, to cover up or stoke a fire, a long mass of cloud or snow, a store or reserve.

MASTERY TEST YEAR 3

[ ] **denotes unit referred to.**

1. Add the correct set of double letters in the space.
pu_____y (tt ll pp) – a young dog **[1]**
2. Add the missing silent letter.
lam____ – a young sheep **[2]**
3. Add the missing vowels.
f___ng___r – part of the hand **[3]**
4. Add the correct letter pattern to complete the word.
b________ (ine ones ane) dogs like to chew them **[4]**
5. Add the correct sound unit to complete the word.
large fish – sh_____k (ir ar er) **[5]**
6. Make this word mean more than **one**.
one **bush** seven __________ **[6]**
7. Add the correct beginning blend.
I baked a loaf of ___ead. (pl bl br) **[7]**
8. Add the correct final blend.
I wore a ma_____ over my face.
(sh sk sh) **[8]**
9. Add **ed** and **ing** to the word 'rub'.
____________ ____________ **[10/11]**
10. What is the base word from which **baking** has come? ____________ **[12]**
11. Join the word parts to make a word that fits the meaning.
The letter is ________________.
(ed + un + open) **[13]**
12. Rearrange the syllables to make a word.
ade lem on (soft drink) ____________ **[14]**
13. Choose the correct spelling of the word in brackets.
The colour of the dress is (blu blue). **[15]**
14. Make two words from the letter pairs which mean a part of the arm and twelve months. ha ye nd ar
__________, __________ **[17]**
15. Use your dictionary to complete this word.
apri____ small orange coloured fruit. **[18]**
16. In **separate** find the name of an animal like a large mouse. __________ **[19]**
17. Circle the correct meaning:
A shape with four sides is called a (circle square house). **[20]**
18. Circle the correct word.
I can (see sea) a camel. **[22]**
19. What is the opposite of **front**?
(rear beside back) **[23]**
20. What word means the same as **hot**?
(old warm cold) **[24]**
21. Circle the simile. He was as white as (coal snow apples). **[25]**
22. Where would you buy a loaf of bread?
(zoo bakery garage) **[26]**
23. Add the correct word.
We played in the hay _______.
(dog stack mill) **[27]**
24. What person makes us laugh?
(doctor clown dentist) **[28]**
25. What is **one** word that could replace the bold words? That puppy is **very unhappy**. (old sad wise) **[29]**
26. Which word belongs to the same group?
dog cow cat (flower pig apple) **[30]**
27. What word rhymes with **slow**?
(light claw go) **[31]**

Many words that we spell have double letters. It is important to know which double letters to add.

Which set of double letters should be added?
The ship was tied to the je_____y. (pp tt rr)
*Answer = The ship was tied to the je**tt**y.*

Choose the correct double letters to complete each word.

1. The ba____oon I blew up burst.
(rr ll tt)

2. Rabbits like to eat ca_____ots.
(pp tt rr)

3. I put the sa_____le on the horse's back.
(dd pp mm)

4. I felt so_____y that Tom couldn't come with us.
(rr pp mm)

5. I have a soft pi_____ow on my bed.
(tt bb ll)

6. Maria made a pu_____et out of paper and wood.
(pp nn dd)

7. Jack stood right in the mi_____le of the circle.
(rr pp dd)

8. I sewed a bu_____on on my shirt.
(tt nn ll)

9. Before I went swimming I put my fli_____ ers on.
(bb pp ss)

10. When I dropped the gla_____, it broke.
(mm ss tt)

11. Mike used some co_____on to sew on the button.
(tt mm nn)

12. The comic book I read was very fu_____y.
(ll tt nn)

SILENT LETTERS

Some words contain letters we do not sound. This can make them difficult to spell.

For example, the word **school** has a silent **h**.

Look at the words in the box. Each has a silent letter.
Circle the letter and write the word in the correct sentence.

crumb	lamb	palm	wrap
wrong	knife	write	know
hour	calf	limb	castle

1. Sixty minutes is one ______________.

2. We cut the meat with a sharp ______________.

3. The hungry bird ate the ______________ of bread.

4. The cow and its ______________ are in the paddock.

5. Are you going to ______________ up the parcel with brown paper?

6. Do you ______________ what time the bus will arrive?

7. A large ______________ tree grew in our backyard.

8. Bill got all his spelling right but I got two ______________.

9. The sheep and its ______________ are in the pen.

10. An arm is a ______________ of your body.

11. A king and queen live in a ______________.

12. Jane is going to ______________ a story about what she did in the holidays.

UNIT 3 THE VOWELS YEAR 4

The vowels are *a* e *i o* and *u*.

Add the missing vowels to make the word.
This m____rn____ng I went for a swim in the pool.
*Answer = This m**o**rn**i**ng I went for a swim in the pool.*

Now add the missing vowels to each of these words.

1. Fiona is my eldest s___st___r.

2. The tow truck p___ll___d the car off the road.

3. The home of a horse is called a st___ bl___.

4. Mike br______ght his new bike to school to show us.

5. A d___nk___y is said to be a stubborn animal.

6. We filled the b___ck___t with water.

7. I put the marbles in my p___ck___t.

8. The goods were made in the large f___ ct___ry.

9. I leant the l___dd___r against the wall so I could climb on to the roof.

10. He climbed from the top to the b____ tt____m of the mountain.

11. Next month our family is going on a long h___l___d___y.

12. A platypus is a strange ___n___m___l.

Many words contain the same group of letters as each other. Recognising these letter patterns helps us learn to spell.

Example

Which word contains the same letter pattern as the bold word?
My father likes to drink ***beer.*** *(stare bare jeer)*
Answer = ***jeer*** *The pattern is* ***eer.***

Now circle the word that contains the same pattern and write the pattern on the line.

1. I bought a loaf of **bread** yesterday.
(snow dead steer)

____

2. I ate a juicy **peach** for my lunch.
(pare glass beach)

____

3. She has a red **rash** on her arm.
(thrash less heat)

____

4. Travis is my best **friend**.
(find spend milk)

____

5. The **mare** and her foal are in the paddock.
(core beer stare)

____

6. It was so hot we jumped in the **pool**.
(hope stool peel)

____

7. We made some **toast** for breakfast.
(soar alone coast)

____

8. The dog ate the **bone.**
(money brood stork)

____

9. The collar on his shirt is **torn**.
(tear nose morning)

____

10. A beautiful **rose** grew in the garden.
(pork whose wire)

____

11. That animal made a strange **sound**.
(ground almost known)

____

12. Last night we had a very heavy **frost.**
(hand float almost)

____

To become good spellers we must know the sounds made by groups of letters.

Example

ai = long **a** sound chain paid
ee = long **e** sound weed sheep

Now choose the correct sound unit to complete each word.

1. We did not know which puppy to ch_____se.
(ai ee oo)

2. This sink is made of stainless st_____l.
(ee oo ai)

3. Every m_____ning before school we go for a run.
(ar or oe)

4. I like to put cr_____m on my strawberries.
(aw ee ea)

5. The teacher told me my watch was made of silv____.
(er ar ie)

6. Did you enj_____ the disco?
(ey oy ay)

7. We made some t_____st for breakfast.
(oe oa ou)

8. When the tiger escaped from its cage I was afr_____d.
(ai au ue)

9. I made a mark on the page with a cr_____on.
(ey oy ay)

10. Our principal made a very long sp_____ch.
(oo ee oe)

11. There is a lot of str _____ in the barn.
(aw ie ir)

12. After the long run I was th _____ sty.
(ar ie ir)

UNIT 6 PLURALS YEAR 4

1. Most words simply add **-s** to make their plurals.
   For example, one **cow** — two **cows**

2. Words that end in **-ch, -sh, -ss, -s** or **-x** make their plurals by adding **-es.**
   For example, one **beach** — two **beaches** one **dress** — two **dresses**

3. Words that end in **-y** before which there is a vowel simply add **-s**.
   For example, one **boy** — two **boys**.
   However, if there is a consonant before the -y then the **-y** is dropped and replaced with an **i** before adding **-es**. For example, one **jelly** — two **jellies**

Make the word in brackets mean more than one.
I had to sew six ____________ in the torn jacket. (stitch)
Answer = I had to sew six ***stitches*** *in the torn jacket.*

Now do these the same way.

1. There are five ____________ on the table. (apple)

2. Callan has four ____________ of grapes. (bunch)

3. I put all of the ____________ on the table. (dish)

4. When I dropped them, the seven ____________ broke. (glass)

5. There are six ____________ in the carpark. (bus)

6. There are over one hundred ____________ on the farm. (turkey)

7. Last week the teacher read us five ____________ about dinosaurs. (story)

8. We picked all the ____________ that were growing in the garden. (poppy)

9. I told her to put all the ____________ in the box. (toy)

10. We saw seven ____________ in the paddock. (fox)

11. The good fairy gave Sharon three ____________. (wish)

12. My cricket team has won all its ____________ this year. (match)

BEGINNING BLENDS

It is important that we are familiar with the groups of letters that are used to begin many words.

Example

Look at the letter groups used to begin these words.

br **br**idge **br**eak **br**own

sn **sn**ail **sn**eak **sn**ore

Write the group of letters that begins the word.

I dug the hole with a ____ade. (tr sp sn)

Answer = I dug the hole with a **spade.**

Now do these. Write the correct letter group in the space.

1. The train pulled into the _____ ation.
(sc st sp)

2. The _____arrow built its nest of leaves and twigs.
(st sp sc)

3. It is rude to _____atch things from others.
(sn tr sw)

4. We saw lots of water birds when we visited the _____amp.
(sc st sw)

5. I pulled the splinter out with some _____ eezers.
(tr tw sw)

6. Roses and daffodils are types of _____ owers.
(fr fl gr)

7. The puppy has _____own a lot since I last saw it.
(gl gr pr)

8. Oona is going to give me my birthday _____esent today.
(pl gr pr)

9. She wore a thick woollen _____arf around her neck.
(sc sk st)

10. I read a story about a fierce _____agon.
(dr pl fl)

11. A dry biscuit is sometimes called a _____ acker.
(cr cl br)

12. There were a lot of _____ossoms on the trees.
(br pl bl)

UNIT 8 FINAL BLENDS YEAR 4

Certain groups of letters are used to end many words.

Look at the letters that end each word in the row.

nd	ba**nd**	le**nd**	fi**nd**	po**nd**
st	la**st**	pe**st**	mi**st**	cru**st**

Choose the final blend that best completes the word.
The tree was blown down by the strong wi_____. (st nd lt)
Answer = The tree was blown down by the strong ***wind****.*

Now do these the same way.

1. I put a sta_____ on the envelope.
   (st nd mp)

2. The sly fox cre_____ silently towards the rabbits.
   (lp nd pt)

3. A tree is a large woody pla_____.
   (st nt mp)

4. That horse is a two-year old co_____.
   (mp lt lp)

5. This teacher is said to be very stri_____.
   (nt nd ct)

6. This old knife is quite blu_____.
   (nt nd st)

7. The tu_____ of an elephant is made of ivory.
   (sk st lt)

8. A deer is a very swi_____ animal.
   (rd ft lt)

9. Last night we had a severe fro_____.
   (sk st ft)

10. Lisa plays a trombo_____ in the school band.
    (mp nd ne)

11. Did you cou_____ all the books?
    (nd nt mp)

12. I am sure Tom's sums are all corre_____.
    (ct st nd)

UNIT 9 — WORD PATTERNS

The shapes of the letters of a word make a pattern.

For example, the letters of **nose** make the pattern n o s e

The letters of **clock** make the pattern c l o c k

Look at the words in the box. Write each in its pattern below.

black	four	mouse	shell
thin	blue	white	frog
sick	park	place	bark

1.

7.

2.

8.

3.

9.

4.

10.

5.

11.

6.

12.

Adding -ed

Certain rules help us become better spellers.

1. When we add **-ed** to the end of many words we do not have to make any changes. For example, play — played
2. If the word ends in a silent **-e** we must drop the **-e** before adding **-ed**. For example, like — liked
3. When we add **-ed** to a word that ends in a short vowel and one consonant we double the consonant before adding **-ed**. For example, hop — hopped

Make the bold word end in **-ed** to fit the sentence.
I ________ goodbye to my friend. ***wave***
Answer = I ***waved*** *goodbye to my friend.*

Now do these the same way.

1. The lady ____________ me a bowl of chips.
(cook)
2. I ____________ the other children my new bike.
(show)
3. I ____________ everywhere for my lost watch.
(look)
4. We all ____________ he would come home soon.
(wish)
5. I really ____________ the way he sang the song.
(like)
6. The dog ____________ the rabbit down its burrow.
(chase)
7. I ____________ the flat tyre on the car.
(change)
8. The lion ____________its prey to a secluded spot.
(drag)
9. We ____________ the plane roar into the sky.
(watch)
10. The car ____________ at the corner.
(stop)
11. It was so cold I ____________ my hands together.
(rub)
12. The horse ____________ past the house.
(trot)

Adding -ing

1. When we add **-ing** to the end of many words we do not have to make any changes. For example, play – playing

2. If the word ends in a silent **-e** we must drop the **-e** before adding **-ing**. For example, dine – dining

3. If the word ends in a short vowel and one consonant we double the consonant before adding **-ing**. For example, drop – dropping

Example

Make the bold word end in **-ing**.
Sam is ____________ up the meat. ***chop***
Answer = Sam is ***chopping*** *up the meat.*

Now do these the same way.

1. Tom is ____________ his friend at noon. (meet)
2. Helen is ____________ a lot of work today. (do)
3. Our choir is ____________ a pretty song. (sing)
4. James is ____________ his horse along the road. (ride)
5. Tommy is ____________ a brand new kite to fly. (make)
6. I am ____________ the money behind this cupboard. (hide)
7. Carly is ____________ across the yard. (skip)
8. The bees are ____________ loudly. (hum)
9. We are ____________ across the pool. (swim)
10. Rajeev is ____________ up the ball of string. (cut)
11. We are going ____________ this afternoon. (shop)
12. I am ____________ the boxes over here. (put)

BASE WORDS

We can add letters to the front or the end of a base word.
For example, from ***cook*** we can add to make ***un**cook**ed***. Note the base word is ***cook.***

Example

Write the base word from which the bold word comes.
*Sally is **hiding** in the bed.*
Answer = **hide**

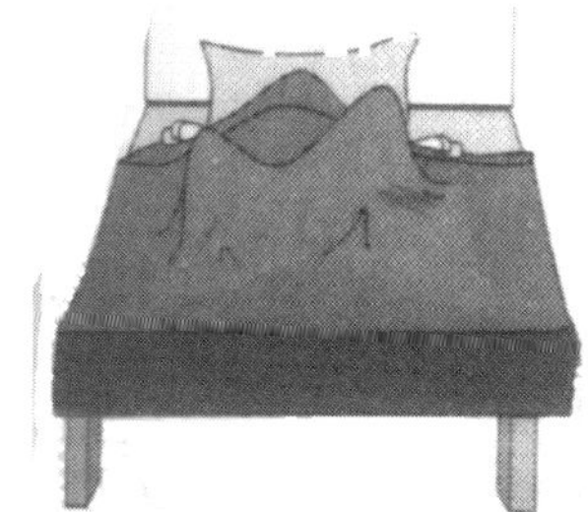

Now do these. Write the base word in the space.

1. Bill was **riding** his horse along the road.

____

2. We were **watching** the football on television.

____

3. The bus **stopped** at the corner.

____

4. When I saw her Sarah was **weeping**.

____

5. Jill has very **curly** hair.

____

6. Ned is **coming** along the road.

____

7. The clothes are **unwashed**.

____

8. We went **indoors** when the rain started.

____

9. This story seems to be **unending**.

____

10. Sadly, the small puppy was **unwanted**.

____

11. This is the **reddest** berry I have seen.

____

12. I put a **spoonful** of sugar in my tea.

____

It helps us spell words if we know they are made up of different parts. These parts are called the *prefix*, the *base word* and the *suffix*.

Example

en	+	*joy*	+	*able*
prefix		*base word*		*suffix*

Rearrange the word parts in the brackets to fit the meaning of the sentence.
The party yesterday was very ____________. (joy en able)
Answer = The party yesterday was very ***enjoyable****.*

Now do these the same way. Underline the prefix and circle the suffix.

1. It was an ________________ game.
(success ful un)

2. Eating too much food is ____________ for you.
(y health un)

3. These clothes are ____________.
(wash un ed)

4. He was ____________ for ten years.
(ed prison im)

5. We went ____________ when the rain began to fall.
(doors in)

6. The teacher ____________ the difficult sum to me.
(plain ex ed)

7. The mushrooms are still ____________ so do not eat them.
(ed un cook)

8. The story Paul is writing is ____________.
(un ed finish)

9. Mel is ____________ to help me.
(ing un will)

10. The treehouse looks ____________.
(stead un y)

11. All these lost clothes and watches are still ____________.
(ed un claim)

12. They are ____________ the house that was destroyed in the fire.
(build re ing)

Every syllable contains a vowel sound. The vowels are a, e, i, o and u.
Sometimes y is used as a vowel, as in happ**y**.

Put the syllables in order so they fit the sentence.
I read the day and date on the ________. (dar en cal)
Answer = I read the day and date on the ***calendar****.*

Now do these the same way.

1. A platypus is a strange ________________.
(i an mal)

2. It is ________________ to run across a road without looking.
(ous ger dan)

3. The children had an exciting ________________ in the city.
(ad ture ven)

4. Are we going to ________________ or stop and have a rest?
(con ue tin)

5. I bought a ________________ about motor bikes.
(mag zine a)

6. I use the ________________ daily.
(tel e phone)

7. A ________________ bit him on the arm.
(qui mos to)

8. The police soon found the ________________ boy.
(a run way)

9. We are going fishing ________________.
(mor to row)

10. Are you going to ________________ me to your friends?
(duce in tro)

11. ________________ is the eleventh month of the year.
(vem No ber)

12. Rebecca always ________________ any pencils she takes.
(re ces pla)

PROOF READING

It is important to be able to recognise whether a word is spelt correctly, simply by looking at it.
Proof reading is an important skill to develop if we are to become good spellers.

Choose the correct spelling of the word.
Jim is standing at the ____________ of the room. (front frount)
Answer = Jim is standing at the ***front*** *of the room.*

Now do these the same way.

1. I wrote a ____________ to my friend in Spain.
(letter leter)

2. There were not ________ lollies left in the jar.
(meny many)

3. We walk to school ________ day of the week.
(evry every)

4. Billy ____________ the glass and it broke.
(droped dropped)

5. We get ________ from a sheep.
(wool wooll)

6. I always eat an ________ for lunch.
(appel apple)

7. He told me he ________ went to England by jet.
(wonce once)

8. Do you want ________ more pie?
(some sum)

9. We walked ____________ the lawn.
(accross across)

10. The ____________ is on the top shelf.
(clok clock)

11. I travelled to Melbourne in a __________.
(train trane)

12. A magpie is a kind of __________.
(burd bird)

DEMON WORDS

Some words constantly cause us spelling problems. We call these Demon Words.

Example

Choose the correct spelling of the Demon Word.
An elephant is big but a mouse is ____________ (littel little)
Answer = An elephant is big but a mouse is ***little****.*

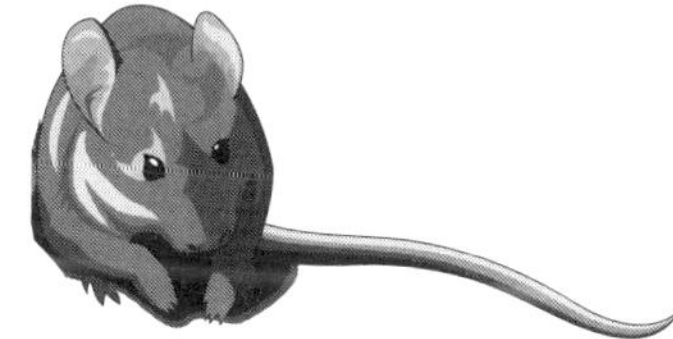

Now do these.

1. We did not know ____________ way to go.
(which whitch)

2. Jim is ____________the first in line.
(always allways)

3. Would you like another ____________ of cake.
(piece perce)

4. Sally did not come ____________ she is ill.
(becorse because)

5. They sewed on the button with ____________.
(cotten cotton)

6. The number after thirty-nine is ____________.
(fourty forty)

7. We went ______________ in the pool.
(swimming swiming)

8. It is ____________ time for us to leave.
(almost allmost)

9. I can see Meg ____________ along the footpath.
(comeing coming)

10. There are lots of children at our ____________.
(skool school)

11. I ____________come with you after all.
(might mite)

12. The thief ____________ to escape through the back door.
(tride tried)

We are able to build new words by adding letters to the front, end or somewhere *inside* a given word.

Example

Add a letter to make a word that fits the sentence.
I bought a kilogram of ________ from the butcher. (mat)
Answer = I bought a kilogram of ***meat*** *from the butcher.*

Now do these the same way.

1. The ____________ drank a lot of water before the journey.
(came)

2. We saw the large ____________ in the forest.
(ear)

3. There was a large ____________ of ships in the harbour.
(feet)

4. The cars must ____________ at the sign.
(top)

5. Bill came last and Jack came ____________ in the race.
(fist)

6. Last night I could hear the croaking of a ____________.
(fog)

7. Cathy is a very ____________ runner.
(fat)

8. A small river is called a ____________.
(steam)

9. The large ____________ was moored at the pier.
(hip)

10. I wore a thick woollen ____________ because it was raining.
(cot)

11. The bird built its ____________ in the tall tree.
(net)

12. We rowed across the lake in a small ____________.
(bat)

USING A DICTIONARY

A dictionary is a useful tool to help us develop spelling skills. We should all learn how to use one. The words in a dictionary are always placed in alphabetical order.

Example

Use your dictionary to help you add the missing letters to the word.
The leader of a team is called a cap_____.
Answer = The leader of a team is called a ***captain****.*

Now use your dictionary to help you do each of these.

1. Something we carry things in is called a **bas** ____________.
2. A male goose is called a **ga**____________.
3. A covering for a bed is a **bla**____________.
4. Another name for an error is a **mis**____________.
5. A small creature with six legs is an **in**____________.
6. Something we put a cup on is called a **sau**____________.
7. A musical instrument with keys is called a **pi**____________.
8. The covering on a bird's body are called **fea**____________.
9. A **chi**____________ removes smoke from a house.
10. A very large person is known as a **gi**____________.
11. The opposite to an answer is called a **que**____________.
12. Something we can draw with is called a **pen**____________.

If we are given pairs of letters we can link them together to make words that fit the meaning of a sentence.

Example

Make two words from the letter pairs in brackets.
There were ________ old ________ on the table. (ha fo ts ur)
Answer = There were ***four*** *old* ***hats*** *on the table.*

Now do these the same way.

1. I am going to ________ Bill a ________ for his birthday.
(bo gi ok ve)

2. I saw a ________ and a ________ in the river.
(fi fr sh og)

3. Alana has a ________ and a ________ to play with.
(ba do ll ll)

4. Jaani's left ________ and his right ________ are covered in mud.
(fo ha ot nd)

5. We get ________ from a sheep and ________ from a cow.
(lk mi ol wo)

6. We played a ________ in the ________.
(me ga ya rd)

7. Susan wore a ________ ________ on her finger.
(go ri ld ng)

8. I bought a warm ________ from the ________.
(sh co op at)

9. I saw a ________ and a ________ when I went to the seaside.
(bo at sh ip)

10. On the ________ I saw a ________.
(fa du rm ck)

11. I ate a ________ and a ________ for my lunch.
(pe ar ke ca)

12. The ________ ate the cheese in the ________.
(tr mi ap ce)

WORD MEANINGS

It is important that you not only know how to spell a word but you must also know its meaning so you can use it correctly.

Circle the correct word.
A small horse is called a
kitten pony kangaroo
Answer = 

Now circle the word that best fits the definition.

1. A person who cares for you when you are in hospital is a (nurse pilot purse).
2. The leader of a team is called the (cabin captain crew).
3. A sweet food made by bees is called (money dozen honey).
4. A very large person is a (ghost giant gander).
5. A hard hat worn to protect the head is called a (helmet helm helped).
6. A type of small red fruit is called a (cherub cherry chair).
7. A type of flower is a (dairy dainty daisy).
8. Something that can be used to make a fire is called a (match market matter).
9. A list of things to eat is called a (mercy mouse menu).
10. A sea creature with eight tentacles is called an (octopus zebra o'clock).
11. Something you would find on a bicycle is called a (pelican pebble pedal).
12. A riding seat on a horse is called a (saddle sandwich sausage).

ANAGRAMS

Anagrams are words we make by rearranging all the letters of another word.

Example

Rearrange the letters to make a word that fits the sentence.
That rabbit is wild, but this one is _________. (meat)
Answer = That rabbit is wild, but this one is ***tame****.*

Now do these.

1. I had a drink of hot ________ with lunch. (eat)

2 Colleen ________ to my house after school. (mace)

3. The little puppy licked its ________. (wasp)

4. I am going to ________ the letter later. (pots)

5. I was sure Mike would win the ________. (care)

6. Two ________ were caught in the trap. (star)

7. The hungry ________ chased the lambs. (flow)

8. Because it has a sore leg the horse is ________. (male)

9. I ate a juicy ________ for lunch. (reap)

10. I was so tired I sat on the ________ all playtime. (east)

11. There was a beautiful ________ bush growing in the garden. (sore)

12. I put the knives and forks on the ________. (bleat)

UNIT 22 HOMOPHONES YEAR 4

Homophones are words that sound the same but have different spellings and different meanings. We often confuse them when we are writing.

Circle the correct word in each sentence.
She asked if I (would wood) like some more cake.
Answer = She asked if I (would) like some more cake.

Now circle the correct word in each sentence below.

1. I received three letters in the (male mail).
2. The (hair hare) was chased by the large dogs.
3. One man is rich and the other is very (poor pour).
4. I threw the orange (peal peel) in the bin.
5. The dog began to (berry bury) the bone in the ground.
6. You dig a (whole hole) with a spade.
7. Mike (through threw) the ball over my head.
8. I will (meet meat) you after school.
9. Be careful you do not (break brake) that glass.
10. I picked a beautiful (rows rose) in the garden.
11. The cowboy rode the (horse hoarse) along the road.
12. In the forest we saw a herd of (dear deer).

ANTONYMS

Antonyms are words that have the opposite, or nearly the opposite, meaning.

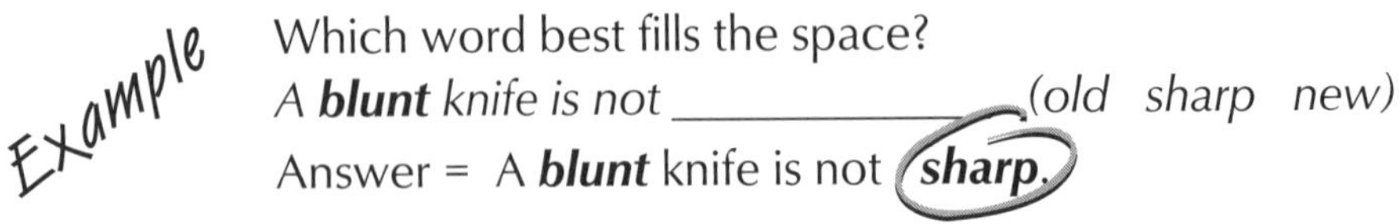

Example

Which word best fills the space?

*A **blunt** knife is not ____________ (old sharp new)*

Answer = A ***blunt*** knife is not ***sharp.***

Now do these. Circle the word that has the opposite meaning.

1. If something is not **alive** it must be (silly old dead).
2. This light is **dull** but that one is (ill bright glad).
3. A person who is **kind** is never (happy tall cruel).
4. If a road is **rough** it is not (pretty cold smooth).
5. A person who is **strong** is not (short ugly weak).
6. If a river is **deep** it is not (shallow hollow kind).
7. This door is **open** but that one is (shut first stupid).
8. Mr Smith is **hairy** but Mr Jones is (bald ripe large).
9. This line is **crooked** but that one is (near clearer straight).
10. This shirt is **clean** but that one is (unripe dirty hilly).
11. Mike is **coming** now but Emmy is (jumping playing going).
12. The watch has been **found** but the pencils are still (safe rude lost).

SYNONYMS

Synonyms are words that have the same, or nearly the same, meaning.

Example

Circle the word that has the same, or nearly the same, meaning.
*This mouse is **small**. (large tiny old)*
Answer = ***tiny***

Now do these.

1. Will you **permit** her to use your bike?
grab tidy allow

2. The clothes are still **damp**.
stuck wet dull

3. That was a **foolish** thing to do.
sensible stupid new

4. The dogs tracked the **smell** of the thief.
footsteps scent jumper

5. I tried hard not to **frighten** the baby rabbit.
knock grab scare

6. This is a **circular** shape.
square round triangular

7. What is the **cost** of that bike?
wheel price colour

8. Mum is going to **mend** my flat tyre.
fix halt mix

9. What time are we going to **begin** the trip?
start end leave

10. Darrell lived on the **border** of the forest.
edge near above

11. Nanna gave me a lovely **gift** for my birthday.
pony shirt present

12. I hope we can **discover** the reason he is so unhappy.
lose find walk

SIMILES

Similes are groups of words used to compare two things. Words such as *as* or *like* are used to make the comparison.

Which word best completes the sentence?
My friend Sally is as wise as an ________.
(bee owl table)
*Answer = My friend Sally is as wise as an **owl**.*

Now do these.

1. The waves looked as big as ____________.
(buildings people ocean)

2. This cloth is as black as ____________.
(night paper ice)

3. When I'm tired I sleep like a __________.
(baby dream person)

4. The stars sparkled like ____________.
(jewels lollies planets)

5. When my Mum's angry she roars like ____________.
(thunder teacher Dad)

6. The wind in the trees moaned like ____________.
(ghosts cyclones trumpets)

7. My mattress feels as hard as ____________.
(rocks beds feathers)

8. My throat feels as dry as ____________.
(sand grass honey)

Now try these. You can use more than one word.

9. The fluffy clouds looked like ________________________.

10. The rain on the roof sounded like ________________________.

11. That big horse is as gentle as ________________________.

12. The cool, white sheets felt like ________________________.

PLACES

Where do people or animals live? Where do we keep or store things? Where do we buy things?

Which word best completes the sentence?
We picked the flowers that were growing in the ____________.
(bedroom garden roof)
Answer = We picked the flowers that were growing in the ***garden****.*

Now do these.

1. I put the letter in the ________________.
(book envelope nest)

2. The bird laid two eggs in the ________________.
(nest basket kettle)

3. Water is boiled in a ________________.
(box kettle cup)

4. You can buy milk in a ________________.
(carton kitten tree)

5. We kept our clothes in the ________________.
(purse kennel wardrobe)

6. I found some coins in an old ________________.
(purse kettle flower)

7. I cooked the food in the ________________.
(bedroom bathroom kitchen)

8. I looked up the meaning of the word in the ________________.
(dictionary bath bushes)

9. We store grain in a ________________.
(silo cup jar)

10. We can buy soft-drinks in a ________________.
(nest bottle match)

11. Wild animals are kept in a ________________.
(sea carton zoo)

12. I bought the food at the ________________.
(supermarket garage cupboard)

COMPOUND WORDS

Compound words are words that are made up of two or more smaller words.

Example

Which word best completes the bold word?
In the park there is a large ***wind*** ________________.
(fruit box mill)
Answer = In the park there is a large ***windmill****.*

Now do these in the same way.

1. I cleaned my teeth with **tooth**________________.
(paper paste cups)

2. I got the letters out of the **mail**________________.
(box cup bell)

3. Robyn said that last night she saw a **space**________________.
(spoon book ship)

4. My pet is a **bull**________________.
(cat mouse dog)

5. Mrs Smith is wearing a pretty **neck**________________.
book lace top)

6. The teacher wrote some words on the **chalk**________________.
(work board fire)

7. I like to play **basket** ________________.
(fast cake ball)

8. I have lots of **home**________________ to do tonight.
(work cost light)

9. Mum parked the car in the **car**________________.
(box port space)

10. There is a high **water**________________ not far from here.
(fall space brush)

11. I ate a delicious **pan**________________ for lunch.
(cake ship bird)

12. We kept walking along the **foot**________________.
(lace dog path)

PEOPLE

People are called different names according to their job or the role they are playing.

Example

Which word best fills the space?
The ________ sold me two loaves of bread.
(butcher baker teacher)
Answer = The ***baker*** *sold me two loaves of bread.*

Now do these in the same way. Write the word in the space.

1. Each year I have my teeth checked by a ________________.
(tailor miner dentist)

2. In the supermarket the money was taken by the ________________.
(doctor butcher cashier)

3. I gave the money for my bus fare to the ____________________.
(teacher nurse conductor)

4. I bought some sausages from the ________________.
(florist butcher newsagent)

5. An older person who frightens younger children is called a ________________.
(magpie bully pilot)

6. The ____________ sentenced the thief to six months in gaol.
(teacher judge miner)

7. A person who investigates crimes is called a __________________.
(footballer detective baker)

8. A person who shoes horses is called a ____________________.
(jockey butcher blacksmith)

9. The ________________ awarded a free kick.
(jockey umpire sailor)

10. The ____________ is now aboard the warship.
(florist sailor artist)

11. The ________________ took my temperature when I was in hospital.
(grocer nurse teacher)

12. The ________________ made me a new suit of clothes.
(doctor judge tailor)

ONE WORD FOR MANY

Often we use a group of words when one word would do instead.

Which word could replace the bold words in the sentence?

The ***young horse*** *ran to the stable. (calf foal piglet)*

Answer = The ***foal*** *ran to the stable.*

Now do these in the same way. Circle the correct answer.

1. Jesse came **after the set time**.
   (soon now late)

2. Mandy was **not very happy**.
   (sad silly laughing)

3. **Find the sum of** the two numbers.
   (take-away add leave)

4. We **washed, dusted, and polished** the car.
   (cleaned chased mowed)

5. Just here the **surface of the earth** is covered in stones.
   (ground tree tables)

6. The house was **the one nearest** to ours.
   (over next under)

7. This is the **way out** of the place.
   (entrance tall exit)

8. Caleb began to **run faster** to get to school.
   (hurry limp play)

9. The monster in the movie was **bad to look at**.
   (pretty big ugly)

10. John took **as much as he needed**.
    (extra none enough)

11. There was a large **group of people** at the match.
    (flock crowd swarm)

12. We walked slowly down the **narrow road.**
    (lane paddock sky)

UNIT 30 CATEGORIES YEAR 4

Many words we use belong to a larger group.

Which word belongs to the same group as the words in bold?
sandals thongs boots *(trainers brown moth)*
Answer = ***trainers***

Now choose the word that belongs to the group.
Write the word in the space.

1. wasp bee ant ________________
(cow fly horse)

2. sparrow robin magpie
____
(emu flower butter)

3. gold silver iron ________________
(paper copper wood)

4. apple plum peach ________________
(coffee orange cake)

5. taxi bus car ________________
(truck kangaroo book)

6. football hockey golf ________________
(petrol umpire soccer)

7. rain hail sleet ________________
(fire road snow)

8. carrots potatoes tomatoes
____
(beans garden banana)

9. shirt frock trousers ________________
(tie leaf cotton)

10. ankle foot toe ________________
(pencil knee hare)

11. chopsticks knife fork ________________
(stove sink spoon)

12. cup plate saucer ________________
(bowl table knife)

HOMOGRAPHS

These are words that have different meanings but exactly the same spelling.

Look how the word ***wave*** can be used.
When she was leaving I began to **wave** to her.
At the beach I saw a large **wave**.

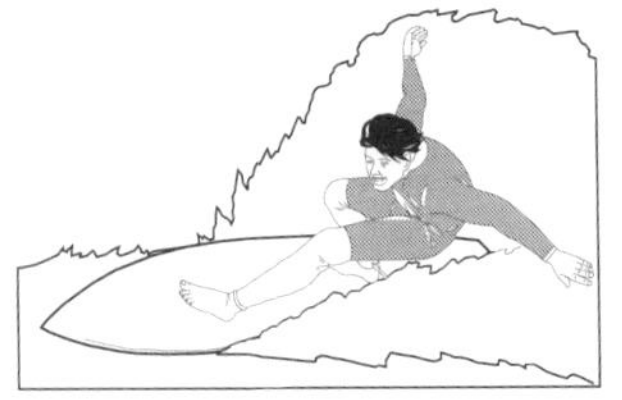

Now use the words to fill the correct spaces below.

rock bank bark trip sink match

1. (a) I could hear the dog ______________ loudly.
   (b) We stripped the ______________ off the tree.

2. (a) Josh threw a ______________ in the creek.
   (b) Be careful not to ______________ the boat.

3. (a) When he dropped it into the water, the heavy cup began to ______________.
   (b) I put all the dishes in the kitchen ______________.

4. (a) We sat and fished from the ______________ of the river.
   (b) I went into the ______________ to get some money.

5. (a) Last week I went to see a cricket ______________.
   (b) After she lit the paper, she blew out the ______________.

6. (a) Be careful you do not ______________over that log.
   (b) We are going on a ______________ to New Zealand next month.

[ ] **denotes unit referred to.**

1. Add the correct set of double letters.
I like to eat je_____y.
(rr ll pp) **[1]**
2. Add the silent letter.
pa_____m (type of tree) **[2]**
3. Add the missing vowels.
w ___nt___r (cold season) **[3]**
4. Add the correct letter pattern.
I ate a p______. (air ear eer) **[4]**
5. Add the correct letter sound.
ch_____n (oo ai ar) **[5]**
6. Make the word **bunch** mean more than one: seven _________________ **[6]**
7. Add the correct beginning blend.
I painted the house _____own.
(tr gl br) **[7]**
8. Add the missing final blend.
I put a sta_____ on the envelope.
(nt mp) **[8]**
9. Add **-ed** and **-ing** to the word 'chase'.
(a) __________ (b) ________ **[10/11]**
10. From what word does **stopping** come?
_________________ **[12]**
11. Rearrange the word parts to make the word. It is (der un stood)
_______________. **[13]**
12. Rearrange the syllables to make the word. (ter yes day) _____________ **[14]**
13. Circle the correct spelling.
Tom is (swimming swiming). **[15/16]**
14. Add a letter to make a word that means a piece of cord. **sting** ____________ **[17]**
15. Use your dictionary to complete this word. A go____________ is a large Australian lizard. **[18]**
16. Make two words to fit the meanings.
bi tr rd ee
woody plant __________
creature with feathers __________ **[19]**
17. Circle the correct word.
A baby horse is called a (fool foal) **[20]**
18. Rearrange the letters of **flow** to get a large dog-like animal. __________ **[21]**
19. Circle the correct word.
Put it over (here hear). **[22]**
20. Which word is the opposite of **bright**?
(shiny dull old) **[23]**
21. Which word means the same as **tidy**?
(silly blue neat) **[24]**
22. Circle the word that completes the saying. I feel as cold as _________.
(cups fire ice) **[25]**
23. Circle the correct word.
A car is kept in a (shed garage). **[26]**
24. Complete the word. There is a large wind_________.
(cup mill) **[27]**
25. Circle the person who cares for your teeth. (doctor dentist teacher) **[28]**
26. What word replaces the bold words?
He is **without hair.**
(ill bald old) **[29]**
27. Which word belongs to the group in bold?
crow, eagle, dove (cow, tree, emu) **[30]**
28. Write some sentences showing the different meanings of **bank**. **[31]**

____

____

____

Notes